D1249702

The Quilt as Art
Rags to Riches

by Laurie Swim

Laurie Swim

ART QUILT PUBLISHING CORPORATION

Art Quilt Publishing Corp., 1356 Blue Rocks Road, RR 1 Lunenburg NS, B0J 2C0 Canada

Also By Laurie Swim:
The Joy of Quilting with an introduction by Alex Colville
Quilting

Library and Archives Canada Cataloguing in Publication
Swim, Laurie
Rags to riches : the quilt as art / Laurie Swim.

ISBN 978-0-9783548-0-0 (bound)

1. Swim, Laurie. 2. Art quilts – Nova Scotia – Lunenburg. 3. Artists' books – Canada. I. Title.

TT835.S874 2007   746.46'0433   C2007-903287-7

For my Mother, Gladys Fiske MacCallum Swim

My special thanks to my husband Larry Goldstein
and his brother Sonny Goldstein; and to our friends, the designers of this book,
Karen and Bob Paul. Without their support, this book would not exist.

Emma's Delight
Collection Museum of Arts & Design, New York, 30"h x 60"w, 1999

Jimmie in His Garden
Private Collecton, 14" x 14", 2006

TABLE *of* CONTENTS

Cover: *Blossom by Blossom*: Collection of the Artist ,15"h x 15"w, 2007

Introduction

My sister makes quilts. Not to sell, but to give to her children and her grandchildren. My mother used to say, "Just watch Barb when she touches fabric. She loves it." And my mother's observation was right. I see Barb's hands lightly move across the surface of a length of woven threads, her fingers feeling what her eyes see, imagining what this weight of cloth, this river of rose may "become". My daughter Barbara paints portraits of fabric, her brush flowing across the canvas transforms that simple backing into silks and satins glowing with textured colours, light caught in folds of velvet, shining through gossamer organzas. My granddaughter, Elizabeth holds a piece of red panne velvet, scrunches it in her fingers, pulls a few threads with her needle and like magic, the petals of a rose open in her hand. The world of fabric – the "idea" of colour made tactile – flowing through the centuries, the most sinuous, delicate and loved of all the "things" that mankind has devised. To give comfort, warmth and delight.

My father said that when his mother finished making a quilt it was considered her most precious gift to the child to whom it was given. And as she had 12 children, the quilts must have been sewn when she could find precious time. Time to give love her children could feel. She might have preferred to read a book. The making of quilts is as much a part of the heritage of women in the new world as the making of bread, or the plucking of chickens, or the careful combining of fat and wood ashes to make soap. All of these activities are within the living memory of those of us who were born in the first 1/3 of the 20th century, and were lucky enough to have come from those busy little settlements scattered like jewels along the headlands and beaches and lakes and rivers of North America. Life was precious, work was hard; but creativity rose up to meet the challenge. And pride of workmanship bestowed a sense of order and polish to an emerging culture. How right that now, when the actual requirement for handmade items no longer exists, that creativity and the desire to add some truth of beauty remain.

It can, perhaps, be argued that much that begins as a requirement for life itself eventually becomes redundant, and then is valued for its aesthetic contribution to life. The paintings of cave dwellers were, we think, meant to give hunters some sense of power over the animals they hoped to slaughter. Not a sport, but a necessity. For centuries we have kept on making paintings – because they satisfy another sort of hunger in humanity.

Detail: *Mermaid's Purse*

And so we come to Laurie Swim's "Quilts". Where do they fit in "the scheme of things?" Are they more akin to the woven or embroidered tapestries from Asia or France and Holland fashioned in the "Middle Ages?" Or are they a development of the geometric or "scrap" quilts made by her thrifty ancestors? Sometimes I think she is so reluctant to leave her own past that she uses her fabric to depict the scenes of a rural way of life from which traditional quilts were made. Neat houses and gardens, barns and fields. But then, as if in a great leap, she sews a virtual tapestry of silks and satins to depict fish – using the best the fabric can offer to give light or life to her canvas. And then, in a sideways leap, she uses her fabrics to celebrate the courage of humanity or the disasters of bad luck.

In all her work, she celebrates. I guess that is her greatest strength, and why I find her work compelling. It is not the careful workmanship she brings to everything she does, nor is it her ability to use colour. It is, rather the evidence we have that she believes in her subjects. She is able to choose fabrics whose textures she understands. And with this understanding she is able to bring warmth and comfort to even the most demanding of her "quilts."

How human and gentle *Breaking Ground* is. And yet she has used the same understanding of line and colours as those artists who created the mosaics on the walls of the Cathedral in Monreale in Sicily, built in the 12th century. Carefully cut bits of gold and gems and stones, pieced together to create a sanctuary that rises around its worshipers with sparkling majesty, each tiny colour caught in the light of hundreds of candle flames.

Hooked rugs employ the same understanding of separating and piecing together colours – making warm and comforting a process which can, when using less forgiving surfaces, become the stuff of formality and worship of the unattainable.

Maybe because fabric is woven, and better understood by humanity than gems, silver, gold or coloured stones that we find it less imposing and somehow easier to accept. The quilt as "wall hanging" or fabric "painting" is tedious to fashion. Beside paintings of similar subjects, it can seem awkward, and somehow not worth the trouble. Is it an art form worth pursuing, or a conceit that is neither painting nor blanket, but a somewhat lesser form of each, with the integrity of neither?

It is not enough to admire the stitches or to say, "How difficult this must have been." No – as any form of creativity it must somehow rise above such considerations, and give us a new form in which we can find some essential part of ourselves we had hitherto not recognized. To merely become a "picture" is not enough. And to be "cute" is unacceptable.

If Laurie Swim were to accept the aesthetic of the abstract, non-representational, it would be easy to place her work beside the work of today's highly acclaimed "textile artists." I recently saw a wall hanging in Canada's National Gallery that was made up of hundreds of items, from small coats cast off from babies to hand bags and men's trousers, all dyed red, all sewn together. Very clever and striking. But Laurie Swim is not a "clever" artist. She does not embrace the "smart". She is as "down home" as the proverbial apple pie. And as a painter who considers jars of jelly, I understand her considerations. It is not easy to remain true to the perceived aesthetics of one's childhood, and at the same time outgrow them. Perhaps it isn't possible. But every artist must be true to whatever images encourage her to take up needle and thread (or brush and paint).

What must come through all of the effort is a way to give confidence to a world that is always in need of reassurance. And whether the result is

Detail: *Breaking Ground*

"smart" or "primitive" or "mundane", it must indicate an understanding of the beautiful. And with luck, it must show love for the human condition.

It is my own observation of artists and their art, that unless there has been significant trauma, some upheaval of tremendous importance in the life of the artist, she can't bring to her creative energy that necessary balance between a peaceful life and one full of great sorrow and impending doom. Experiencing these extremes as Laurie Swim has done, has given her a choice. What to celebrate? What to complain about?

Laurie Swim has not chosen to complain. Her wall hangings are as full of optimism as she must have had when, as a child, she ventured into a field of wild flowers or looked with amazement from a headland at the expanse of sea lying beyond her.

And so, as she has chosen to celebrate her world, so do I honour her quilts.

Mary Pratt ~ April 24, 2007

Back Yards, Where We Live

Back Yards, Where We Live is a series of works produced on and off over a ten year period from 1997-2007. In 1989, we had moved from midtown Toronto to the countryside outside Kingston, Ontario. After writing my second book, *Quilting* in 1991, I diverged from making quilt art and explored felt making as a medium. I also created editions of etchings in printmaking. In 1995, I took up quilt art again and in 1998, we moved back to Toronto and from there to Nova Scotia in 2004. This series of works in many ways documents those years. In 2003, before leaving Ontario, I was awarded a Chalmers Fellowship from the Ontario Arts Council to complete my series, *Back Yards, Where We Live*.

From Our Back Yard

The first piece, *From Our Back Yard*, (page 12) is a view behind the home we had in the countryside just north of the university town of Kingston in eastern Ontario, Canada. We lived in this rural setting for eight years surrounded by a diversity of neighbours; university professors, old Loyalist families and long time farmers.

The view in which the work is shaped included our own back yard and the adjacent farmhouse. Our house was a converted church built on bedrock in 1878. It is referenced by the gothic window in the farmhouse that in reality did not exist in that structure. This work recorded an intimate scene, one familiar to all, a back yard with laundry on the line.

Commercially printed fabric images of the farmer and farm animals are hidden within the background surrounding the farmhouse. In this work I used fabric paint for the first time to create shadow and highlights in the piece. I was especially pleased with the basket which was painted with dashes of an opaque yellow over a floral print. The chairs were also highlighted with transparent fabric paint and appliquéd by hand. I used "cobweb lace" to create the foliage in the trees. This method of compiling many small bits of fabric for foliage has been consistent throughout the *Back Yards* series.

Emma's Delight

Emma's Delight, (page 4) from that time and locale, depicts our beloved family dog frolicking in the farmer's field across the road from our home. We actually inherited Emma from the previous owners of the property. She took up her role immediately as nanny to my son, then four, as his constant companion and guardian. As well as the quilt I made an etching of the same scene, *Across the Road*, that included my son. *Emma's Delight* is in the permanent collection of The Museum of Arts & Design in New York City. It was part of the *Six Continents of Quilts* exhibition by the Museum, first shown at the Paine-Webber USB gallery in New York City July – September 2002 and traveled on tour around the world until 2006.

Nova Scotia Homestead

Next came *Nova Scotia Homestead*, (page 14) a depiction of the side yard of a heritage property in the town of Lockeport, Nova Scotia where I spent my childhood and where most of my family still lives. I am long acquainted with its history.

It is one of five homes, all next to each other, built between 1836 and 1878 by my Locke ancestors, for whom the town is named. This grouping of houses is registered as a provincial heritage site. There are three architectural styles represented; Cape Cod, Regency and Victorian. Known as *The Locke Family Streetscape* they can be found along the waterfront in Lockeport.

While I was still living in Kingston, I made an etching of the streetscape. The yard of the house I have depicted as the quilted work, *Nova Scotia Homestead* is the Regency house in the middle of the five.

My childhood friend, the present owner, inherited this property from her grandparents who emigrated from Denmark after the First World War. Our grandmothers were friends and our mothers were very close as young women and throughout their adult lives. We played together along with her younger sister, as children in the back yard and revisit it as adults. The charms of the past and present have merged together in this piece.

For the siding on the house, a printed striped fabric was turned to the back and then the lines machine quilted. The area under the eaves is the front of the striped fabric and has been painted with a wash of purple to emphasize the shadow. There are more painted shadows on the fence, as well as the door of the house and garage. To create the screen in the door, I applied a blue organza. Many cotton prints in green were used for the leafy foliage.

At the End of the Day

At the End of the Day (page 16) was the view of the alley behind our upper duplex in an old established Italian neighbourhood in Toronto, Ontario where we lived after moving back to the city in 1998. This urban view was a great contrast to the rural setting of *From Our Back Yard*. The alleyway divided the residential area from backs of storefront properties on a main street. This configuration is found universally in city settings. The alley never looked as good as it did in latter daylight. Reflective light and long shadows created a magical mysterious quality. Rarely is a cityscape without people so I added the figure of a woman to make the scene less ominous.

After the quilt was completed I noticed that in the centre of the piece between the tree trunks, there was a small patch of fabric that appeared to be the likeness of two kittens peeping out from behind a building in the alley. There were always feral cats in the alley. This added gift out of the blue gave the work a life and charm of its own beyond my own intention.

The sky was hand dyed by me and machine quilted. Shadows for the stairs of the fire escape were created by layers cut from black tulle. *At the End of the Day* has garnered a lot of attention at quilt shows with Viewers' Choice Awards and even as recently as 2007, the cover of an international quilting magazine.

A Farewell

In 2004, as a respite from city living and stress we had endured for the past year with my fight with cancer, my husband and I decided to rent a little house in Blue Rocks, Nova Scotia for the summer. A photograph was sent to us over the internet of a small white house with blue shutters and a five sided dormer that sits on the roof overhanging the front porch known as the 'Lunenburg bump'. We had no sense of the property or what it looked upon. All we knew was that Blue Rocks was an enchanting fishing settlement on the headland just beyond Lunenburg; anywhere in that area would likely be lovely. On our arrival at the house the reality of our surroundings surpassed

The Stricklands of Blue Rocks

any conjured fantasy. The view in *A Farewell* (page 18) is what our little fisherman's cottage looked upon, the neighboring house and Sand Cove beyond that.

My first impression of this graciously proportioned building was that the image is reminiscent of an Edward Hopper painting. The American painter captured the magnificent light of the East Coast that has also influenced me and many other visual artists. The elusive and fleeting light, caused by the reflections of sky on water that surrounds us here on the coast sometimes causes me to respond emotionally; its beauty just "breaks your heart". You want to hang onto it forever. As homage to Hopper I have included the figure in the bay window from his painting, *Cape Cod Morning*.

As the summer passed in Sand Cove, we met our neighbours next door; Louise and Clayton and they became our friends. Clayton, a retired sea captain could always be counted on for a yarn of local history and Louise made a lemon meringue pie that captured my husband's heart. Autumn rolled around and we decided to stay in Blue Rocks and not return to the city. I had come home.

In the Fall of 2005, a year and half after our moving to Blue Rocks, Clayton fell ill and passed on within six weeks. He knew he was dying and in those weeks, their driveway was full of cars of friends coming to say their good-byes. His spirit still is with us in the little drawing I did of him, the figure in the piece standing off from the right of the house. *A Farewell* is not only a goodbye but a gesture that expresses that we wish a happy journey, whatever it might be, for those who touch us and then take their leave.

This work is made of mostly cotton fabric, some of which has been recycled from scraps made into "cobweb lace". The sky is hand painted and so are the flowers in the foreground. The figures are original drawings scanned, printed on fabric, hand tinted and appliquéd. The shadow of the house was created with transfer paint on paper that was then cut in the shape of the shadow, placed on the house and heat-transferred with an iron.

Mermaid's Purse

This work came about one day when I was passing by a house overlooking Lunenburg Harbour. The clothes on the line and the dragger in the bay together told me a story that inspired *Mermaid's Purse*. (page 20)

After many days at sea the fisherman arrived home in the night to a warm body and bed. On this Monday morning the old tomcat is returning after a night of hunting on the shore. The fisher's wife has risen early to do her wash. The flimsy nightie on the line indicates all is well between man and wife. He has returned safe once again.

This piece represents a way of life that has almost disappeared on the Eastern Seaboard of the North Atlantic with the demise of the fishing industry in recent years. Many of the men loved being on the open water, seduced by the adventure and the independence it gave them. It was hard work as well, so when in shore, they wanted only rest and relaxation. 'Going to sea' has always been a dangerous profession. On the home front, the women were always on the lookout for the safe return of their menfolk, not just husbands, but also sons, brothers and neighbours, for they tended to work together. The railed deck above the windowed porch, a 'widow's walk', allows a view to the distant horizon on the ocean.

The enigmatic title refers to the black shape on the clothes line which could be a man's shirt. In this work, however, it is a representation of a mermaid's purse, which is the common name for an egg sack of the skate fish. The subtext of this work is that the wife in a fisher's family traditionally managed the financial affairs of the household since her husband was often away at sea. His share of the proceeds of the catch would be handed over to her to budget.

The sky and water were hand painted on recycled cotton sheets. The piece was mostly created with cotton and some silk fabrics. The bushes in the foreground and trees on the far hillside used a lot of cobweb lace. The cat was fashioned out of black velvet. This work was done with the assistance of Clarissa Waldron.

Bygones

I love the architectural style of the Cape Cod house. To me it represents both simplicity and elegance. It is one of the earliest structures built on these shores. As in this example, many were added on to, either by repeating the same shape alongside, or by adding the addition as an L.

Beyond Blue Rocks is Stonehurst, another early settlement known locally as Black Rocks. Stonehurst North and Stonehurst South point out into the ocean on the two fingers of Schooner Bay. This structure is on Stonehurst South. One day as I was making my way along this enchanting twisting path of road, I spotted the double Cape with its row of seagulls taking in the last moments of the day together. The scene captured my visual heart. I knew it was going to be a special piece for me from the start; the soft turquoise of the fading light, the weathered building with the overgrown pathway and the line of birds, the frosting.

Bygones (page 22) bridges the gap between the two series of works, *Back Yards, Where We Live* and *The Ragged Shore*. I didn't create the series linearly; that is, I worked on both after I moved to Nova Scotia. The rawness to the materials I used to create the *Ragged Shore* pieces, which are made on a smaller scale, are mostly of scraps of silk and feathered hairy yarns, perfect for depicting the flavour and texture of the landscape hereabouts. For *Bygones*, I used those same elements on a larger scale. I constructed the houses from some printed cottons, some upholstery fabrics and brocaded silks to replicate the reflection of the sun on an old building.

For the overgrown path, I painted earth pastels on a recycled sheet and covered it with sparkling green gold organza and proceeded to stitch and machine embroider long grasses. There is much overlaid stitching of grass and underbrush on the sides of the path with a line of hairy yarns in red to add to the texture. There is cobweb lace here and there, bits of sparkling Angelina Fibers in the foliage and even fabric I sun-printed with ferns, creating a bush near the right side of the house.

The birds crowned the work. I fashioned them out of a metallic silk organza. When the work was finished and on display, a friend told me that when you see a row of birds such as this, there is always one bird that acts as a lookout in the opposite direction. Sure enough, I had unconsciously turned one of the birds the other way. Serendipity has always been my friend.

Magic Hour, Blue Rocks and *Where Angels Play*
Magic hour describes the time just before the sun sets, when it sits just above the horizon and casts elusive light parallel to the land turning windows into gold reflections and breaking up the water into silver slivers. This scene of Sand Cove is very near where we live. Sea vistas, rugged shoreline and atypical maritime historical architecture come together in *Magic Hour, Blue Rocks*. (page 24)

Blue Haven Rd.

Where Angels Play (page 26) is a larger version of much the same scene as *Magic Hour* but is portrayed at a slightly different angle. It has added details such as the boat in the water of the cove. There are cherubim hiding in the bushes at the side of the house and near the waters edge. The red 'fish store' shack has been shifted a little ways to the left to reveal the back yard in this piece.

The wooded area in back of the house is more mysterious. It is the same woods as behind our house in Blue Rocks just up from the cove. I have seen as many as eight deer at one time in our back yard. On a regular basis, a handsome emerald green and rust male pheasant makes his appearance known with a loud obnoxious squawk. I spotted a fox once nestled into a rise of undergrowth. These visitors are always a welcome surprise to me after many years of living in an urban setting.

In both works, I have used layers of organza over other fabrics to create the water and the reflection. The shadows on the house are created with chiffon and sheer organza overlays. The spruce trees are roughly cut tree shapes free machine embroidered. There are both spun sari silk and hairy yarns in the field areas. Hand dyed fabric was used to create the granite rocky shore.

From Our Back Yard
Collection Lori and David Rousseau, 56"h x 52"w, 1997

Nova Scotia Homestead
Collection John Risely, 58"h x 48"w, 2007

At the End of the Day
Collection of the Artist, 48"h x 54"w, 2002

A Farewell
Collection of the Artist, 62"h x 55"w, 2006

Mermaid's Purse
Collection of the Artist, 52"h x 60"w, 2006

Bygones
Collection of the Artist, 45"h x 60"w, 2006

Magic Hour, Blue Rocks
Collection of the Artist, 25"h x 25"w, 2005

Where Angels Play
Collection of the Artist, 48"h x 56"w, 2007

The Ragged Shore

The Ragged Shore is inspired by the rugged coastline of southwest Nova Scotia. I grew up in Lockeport, a seaside town. I graduated from the Nova Scotia College of Art and Design in 1971. My first success as an artist was here. In 1976, I was awarded Best in Show at the annual Nova Scotia Designer Craftsman Exhibition. Alex Colville was the juror. He contributed the introduction to my first book, *The Joy of Quilting*, in 1984.

Like many Nova Scotians, I moved to another part of Canada as a young woman. Nova Scotia's pull on me was very strong, however. During all those years away, from 1977 on, I visited at least once a year. Much of my work done in Ontario reflected the Nova Scotia landscape and my heritage.

In 2003, I was asked to come to Nova Scotia for the summer in order to create a work for the 250th anniversary of the founding of Lunenburg, about 70 miles up the coast from Lockeport. When I wasn't working on the *Lunenburg Heritage Quilt*, I was exploring the low-lying fingers of headlands pointing into the sea. Left by the last ice age, long striations of granite

outcroppings appear in the landscape with spruce and other plant life clinging miraculously to their surfaces. The stunted undergrowth surrounding them is thick and rich with texture and colour. Simple geometric wooden structures crop up, nestled in coves, often protected by a surround of windbreak trees. Sometimes these structures face the Atlantic, welcoming, and at the same time defiant, of all that comes their way.

This imagery is great stuff for an artist, especially one who loves fibre as well as the texture of the landscape. When I returned to the city that autumn, I felt not just a heightened awareness of this landscape but something even more intrinsic; déjà vu tinged with genetic ancestral memories, a deeper understanding of what has come before and my connection to it. This was the beginning of a new direction in my work. I started work on *At the Point*, (page 30) a piece inspired by what is called simply The Point, in Blue Rocks. It became the first in the series, *The Ragged Shore*.

In 2004 my husband and I came back to spend the summer in Nova Scotia. We rented a little house in Blue Rocks, just beyond Lunenburg. I started doing sketches in charcoal on textured board. These drawings were to become the studies for the future works in fabric and thread. The black charcoal on white surfaces eliminated colour and allowed me to explore the strata and the contrast of the landscapes. It was in this manner that I became intimately acquainted with the subject matter.

When Autumn rolled around, we could not leave the beauty and tranquility of Blue Rocks for the noise and grit of the city. We had given up our apartment in Toronto and put our possessions in storage, in anticipation of our return in the Fall. Instead, we sent for our belongings. I began rendering the drawings in fabric.

Stonehurst Houses, (page 31) *Stonehurst Cape,* (page 32) *Blue Boats in Blue*

Rocks, (page 33) *Sand Cove,* (page 34) and *Sand Cove, Fish Store* (page 35) depict the terrain in Stonehurst and Blue Rocks. *LaHave Evening* (page 36) is a location on the La Have River nearby. *Ocean View,* (page 37) *Over the Hill to Nana Kay's,* (page 38) *West Head* (page 39) and *Ragged Isle* (page 40) are scenes from Lockeport and surrounding area. All started out as sketches.

The two Stonehurst pieces and *Blue Boats in Blue Rocks,* an homage to a disappearing way of life, depict the historical relationship between people and the sea. In the case of *Sand Cove* and *Sand Cove, Fish Store,* I created two fabric works of the same view of the fish store in Sand Cove but portrayed a different time of day with each of them.

Ocean View depicts the front yard of one of the homes in Lockeport that is part of the provincial heritage site, The Locke Family Streetscape. My father's sister, my aunt Lillian, lived in this house by the sea. I remember one evening stepping off the front porch, rarely used to enter the house, onto the lawn which was mostly soft moss. I had the eerie feeling I had stepped back in time and retreated to the safety of the house. From then on, I used the back entrance which felt much friendlier. In this work, I have tried to capture the timeless moment of the last glow of the day reflected on the house and the property surrounding it with bright silks for the lawn and silver metallic thread on the tree trunk. For the yellow light on the house, I have used a scrap of chiffon scarf.

Over the Hill to Nana Kay's is a view from my family home to my paternal grandmother's place in Lockeport. There was once a well worn path here. Nana Kay's property is no longer in the family. The hill that connects the two houses has become overgrown. Here, I tried to convey nature's texture with bits of silk in the range of colour found in this landscape.

Ragged Isle is a vista of an island close to the shore across Lockeport's Crescent Beach . It once was used for grazing sheep, holding them without fences. The

trees are free motion machine embroidered. The rocks on the right foreground shore are stitched and enhanced with touches of acrylic paint.

West Head was done from a sketch I did many years ago of the view from my parent's living room in Lockeport towards West Head across the way. I had been fascinated with the late day light on the spruce trees and their trunks. Another thing I wanted to capture in the work was the many colours of the vegetation in the field between the house and the shore. *Cat Spruce Survivor* (page 41) is a smaller similar example of my attempt to capture the essence of that environment.

The study for *Stonehurst Fish Store,* (page 42) started out as a small line drawing in ink on paper. Beads represent gravel and rocks. There is free motion embroidery over hand dyed fabric to depict the yellow seaweed and trees lining the shore. The scene is surrounded by a border of lilac silk.

Dublin Shore (page 43) also started as a line drawing. This scene is along the LaHave River. In the autumn of 2006, my husband and I decided we would explore all the roads we hadn't been down before, mostly side tracks that come to dead ends off the main roads. It was very exciting. We would come upon views of astounding peace and beauty. I had a new camera and took lots of photographs for future reference. I have material for images for years to come. *Dublin Shore* embodies a lot of what I have tried to convey with the *Ragged Shore* series, the texture of the landscape, the stalwart and simple structures and the rugged shoreline.

Sketch for *Dublin Shore,* page 43.

At the Point
Collection Tom Mason, 16"h x 27"w, 2004

Stonehurst Houses
Collection Robert and Barbara Hunter, 17"h x 32"w, 2007

Stonehurst Cape
Collection Jane Alexander and Ed Sherin, 15"h x 32"w, 2005

Blue Boats in Blue Rocks
Collection Dr. Deborah Thompson, 19"h x 32"w, 2005

Sand Cove
Private Collection, 18"h x 32"w, 2005

Sand Cove, Fish Store
Private Collection, 18"h x 32"w, 2005

LaHave Evening
Collection of the Artist, 16"h x 32"w, 2005

Ocean View
Private Collection, 18"h x 30"w, 2002

Over the Hill to Nana Kay's
Collection Ron Cotton, 16"h x 27"w, 2004

West Head
Collection Ron Cotton, 18"h x 14"w, 2004

Ragged Isle
Collection Marie and Bill Clarke, 15"h x 27"w, 2004

Cat Spruce Survivor
Collection Katherine Osler and Paul Kellogg, 9"h x 11"w, 2004

Stonehurst Fish Store

Collection Nova Scotia Art Bank, 15"h x 15"w, 2005

Dublin Shore
Collection of the Artist, 17"h x 32"w, 2007

The Blue Rocks Yacht Club

Picasso had his Blue Period. I have Blue Rocks.

In the summer of 2004 I returned to Nova Scotia and the coastline I know so well that it came to me in vivid detail in dreams during all the 30 years I lived away. Most of this shoreline was formed by the last ice age. It is made up of striations of rock covered in mossy outcroppings and craggy spruce, wind-beaten by the sea gales of the Atlantic. Blue Rocks is a tiny fishing community near Lunenburg, huddled on a finger of land pointing southeast into the Atlantic Ocean.

They are called fish stores. Fish stores, I soon learned from a retired neighbouring fisherman, is not where you buy fish but where a fisher keeps his gear and baits his lines. In the past and the present, these out-buildings have also served as singularly male refuges from domesticity.

Blue Rocks and neighbouring Stonehurst have many fish stores still in use, many of them conveniently located near to the house of the owner. When these land lots were first parcelled out, the family was given a water right-of-way as well. The rights-of-way for the original properties in Blue Rocks still exist today. In the warmer season, there are many small leisure craft, dories and the like, as well as Cape Island boats, anchored in this small cove. This fish store, now heritage-designated, affectionately referred to by us locals as the Blue Rocks Yacht Club, is probably the most photographed building of its kind in Nova Scotia.

In the past I wondered, "Why would anyone build a home in such a remote area?" Now I understand that originally there weren't roads, there was only the seaway. In those early times, the sea not only provided a livelihood but transported you to work, to supplies and to other outlying communities. The fish store is the remnant of that way of life.

Every day that first summer I looked out the window of the little house we rented there, and saw Sand Cove with its weathered little building sitting on a rock outcrop surrounded by bright yellow seaweed. Outlying Nova Scotia fishing communities are peppered with these shacks. They serve the inshore fishermen as moorings for their Cape Island boats.

Recreating this simple exquisite weathered structure became the focus for a series of small works. The result is a journal of enchanting faces of the shore and the ever-changing light in the sky and water I encountered over the past years. The allure will continue as long as I have the privilege to live here.

BlueDay In Blue Rocks
Private Collection, 12"h x 9"w, 2004

First Snow, Blue Rocks
Collection Stephanie Lever, 12"h x 8"w, 2004

Sand Cove Dresses Up
Collection George and Janet Palmer, 12"h x 8"w, 2004

Storm Warning
Collection Jane Alexander and Ed Sherin, 12"h x 10"w, 2005

Fish Store in Fog Surround
Collection Sondra Bolton, 10"h x 10"w, 2004

Late Autumn Glow
Private Collection, 11"h x 12"w, 2004

Fog at Dusk, Sand Cove
Collection Bob and Karen Paul, 12"h x 12"w, 2004

Blue Rocks Yacht Club
Collection Katherine Osler and Paul Kellogg, 13"h x 12"w, 2004